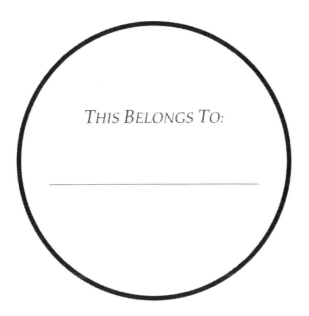

THIS BELONGS TO:

_____

DATE: _____/_____/_____

I am grateful for...

1. _____
2. _____
3. _____

My goals for today are...

1. _____
2. _____
3. _____

My motivation for today is...

_____

_____

These wonderful things happened today...

1. _____
2. _____
3. _____

How did I make these things happen?

_____

_____

_____

DATE: ____/____/____

I am grateful for...

1. _____

2. _____

3. _____

My goals for today are...

1. _____

2. _____

3. _____

My motivation for today is...

_____

_____

These wonderful things happened today...

1. _____

2. _____

3. _____

How did I make these things happen?

_____

_____

_____

DATE: _____/_____/_____

I am grateful for...

1. _____

2. _____

3. _____

My goals for today are...

1. _____

2. _____

3. _____

My motivation for today is...

_____

_____

These wonderful things happened today...

1. _____

2. _____

3. _____

How did I make these things happen?

_____

_____

_____

DATE: ____/____/____

I am grateful for...

1._____
2._____
3._____

My goals for today are...

1._____
2._____
3._____

My motivation for today is...

_____

_____

These wonderful things happened today...

1._____
2._____
3._____

How did I make these things happen?

_____

_____

_____

DATE: _____/_____/_____

I am grateful for...

1. _____

2. _____

3. _____

My goals for today are...

1. _____

2. _____

3. _____

My motivation for today is...

_____

_____

These wonderful things happened today...

1. _____

2. _____

3. _____

How did I make these things happen?

_____

_____

_____

DATE: _____/_____/_____

I am grateful for...

1. _____

2. _____

3. _____

My goals for today are...

1. _____

2. _____

3. _____

My motivation for today is...

_____

_____

These wonderful things happened today...

1. _____

2. _____

3. _____

How did I make these things happen?

_____

_____

_____

DATE: ____/____/____

I am grateful for...

1. _____
2. _____
3. _____

My goals for today are...

1. _____
2. _____
3. _____

My motivation for today is...

_____

_____

These wonderful things happened today...

1. _____
2. _____
3. _____

How did I make these things happen?

_____

_____

_____

DATE: _____/_____/_____

I am grateful for...

1._____
2._____
3._____

My goals for today are...

1._____
2._____
3._____

My motivation for today is...

_____

_____

These wonderful things happened today...

1._____
2._____
3._____

How did I make these things happen?

_____

_____

_____

DATE: _____/_____/_____

I am grateful for...

1. _____

2. _____

3. _____

My goals for today are...

1. _____

2. _____

3. _____

My motivation for today is...

_____

_____

These wonderful things happened today...

1. _____

2. _____

3. _____

How did I make these things happen?

_____

_____

_____

DATE: _____/_____/_____

I am grateful for...

1._____

2._____

3._____

My goals for today are...

1._____

2._____

3._____

My motivation for today is...

_____

_____

These wonderful things happened today...

1._____

2._____

3._____

How did I make these things happen?

_____

_____

_____

DATE: ____/____/____

I am grateful for...

1. _____
2. _____
3. _____

My goals for today are...

1. _____
2. _____
3. _____

My motivation for today is...

_____

_____

These wonderful things happened today...

1. _____
2. _____
3. _____

How did I make these things happen?

_____

_____

_____

DATE: _____ / _____ / _____

I am grateful for...

1. _____

2. _____

3. _____

My goals for today are...

1. _____

2. _____

3. _____

My motivation for today is...

_____

_____

These wonderful things happened today...

1. _____

2. _____

3. _____

How did I make these things happen?

_____

_____

_____

DATE: _____/_____/_____

I am grateful for...

1. _____
2. _____
3. _____

My goals for today are...

1. _____
2. _____
3. _____

My motivation for today is...

_____

_____

These wonderful things happened today...

1. _____
2. _____
3. _____

How did I make these things happen?

_____

_____

_____

DATE: _____ / _____ / _____

I am grateful for...

1. _____
2. _____
3. _____

My goals for today are...

1. _____
2. _____
3. _____

My motivation for today is...

_____

_____

These wonderful things happened today...

1. _____
2. _____
3. _____

How did I make these things happen?

_____

_____

_____

DATE: _____/_____/_____

I am grateful for...

1. _____
2. _____
3. _____

My goals for today are...

1. _____
2. _____
3. _____

My motivation for today is...

_____

_____

These wonderful things happened today...

1. _____
2. _____
3. _____

How did I make these things happen?

_____

_____

_____

DATE: _____/_____/_____

I am grateful for...

1._____

2._____

3._____

My goals for today are...

1._____

2._____

3._____

My motivation for today is...

_____

_____

These wonderful things happened today...

1._____

2._____

3._____

How did I make these things happen?

_____

_____

_____

DATE: _____ / _____ / _____

I am grateful for...

1. _____

2. _____

3. _____

My goals for today are...

1. _____

2. _____

3. _____

My motivation for today is...

_____

_____

These wonderful things happened today...

1. _____

2. _____

3. _____

How did I make these things happen?

_____

_____

_____

DATE: _____ / _____ / _____

I am grateful for...

1. _____
2. _____
3. _____

My goals for today are...

1. _____
2. _____
3. _____

My motivation for today is...

_____

_____

These wonderful things happened today...

1. _____
2. _____
3. _____

How did I make these things happen?

_____

_____

_____

DATE: _____ / _____ / _____

I am grateful for...

1. _____

2. _____

3. _____

My goals for today are...

1. _____

2. _____

3. _____

My motivation for today is...

_____

_____

These wonderful things happened today...

1. _____

2. _____

3. _____

How did I make these things happen?

_____

_____

_____

DATE: _____/_____/_____

I am grateful for...

1. _____

2. _____

3. _____

My goals for today are...

1. _____

2. _____

3. _____

My motivation for today is...

_____

_____

These wonderful things happened today...

1. _____

2. _____

3. _____

How did I make these things happen?

_____

_____

_____

DATE: ____/____/____

I am grateful for...

1. _____
2. _____
3. _____

My goals for today are...

1. _____
2. _____
3. _____

My motivation for today is...

_____

_____

These wonderful things happened today...

1. _____
2. _____
3. _____

How did I make these things happen?

_____

_____

_____

DATE: ___/___/___

I am grateful for...

1._____

2._____

3._____

My goals for today are...

1._____

2._____

3._____

My motivation for today is...

_____

_____

These wonderful things happened today...

1._____

2._____

3._____

How did I make these things happen?

_____

_____

_____

DATE: _____/_____/_____

I am grateful for...

1. _____
2. _____
3. _____

My goals for today are...

1. _____
2. _____
3. _____

My motivation for today is...

_____

_____

These wonderful things happened today...

1. _____
2. _____
3. _____

How did I make these things happen?

_____

_____

_____

DATE: _____/_____/_____

I am grateful for...

1._____

2._____

3._____

My goals for today are...

1._____

2._____

3._____

My motivation for today is...

_____

_____

These wonderful things happened today...

1._____

2._____

3._____

How did I make these things happen?

_____

_____

_____

DATE: _____/_____/_____

I am grateful for...

1. _____

2. _____

3. _____

My goals for today are...

1. _____

2. _____

3. _____

My motivation for today is...

_____

_____

These wonderful things happened today...

1. _____

2. _____

3. _____

How did I make these things happen?

_____

_____

_____

DATE: _____/_____/_____

I am grateful for...

1._____

2._____

3._____

My goals for today are...

1._____

2._____

3._____

My motivation for today is...

_____

_____

These wonderful things happened today...

1._____

2._____

3._____

How did I make these things happen?

_____

_____

_____

DATE: _____ / _____ / _____

I am grateful for...

1. _____
2. _____
3. _____

My goals for today are...

1. _____
2. _____
3. _____

My motivation for today is...

_____

_____

These wonderful things happened today...

1. _____
2. _____
3. _____

How did I make these things happen?

_____

_____

_____

DATE: ___/___/___

I am grateful for...

1. _____
2. _____
3. _____

My goals for today are...

1. _____
2. _____
3. _____

My motivation for today is...

_____

_____

These wonderful things happened today...

1. _____
2. _____
3. _____

How did I make these things happen?

_____

_____

_____

DATE: ____/____/____

I am grateful for...

1. _____

2. _____

3. _____

My goals for today are...

1. _____

2. _____

3. _____

My motivation for today is...

_____

_____

These wonderful things happened today...

1. _____

2. _____

3. _____

How did I make these things happen?

_____

_____

_____

DATE: _____/_____/_____

I am grateful for...

1._____

2._____

3._____

My goals for today are...

1._____

2._____

3._____

My motivation for today is...

_____

_____

These wonderful things happened today...

1._____

2._____

3._____

How did I make these things happen?

_____

_____

_____

DATE: _____/_____/_____

I am grateful for...

1. _____

2. _____

3. _____

My goals for today are...

1. _____

2. _____

3. _____

My motivation for today is...

_____

_____

These wonderful things happened today...

1. _____

2. _____

3. _____

How did I make these things happen?

_____

_____

_____

DATE: _____/_____/_____

I am grateful for...

1. _____

2. _____

3. _____

My goals for today are...

1. _____

2. _____

3. _____

My motivation for today is...

_____

_____

These wonderful things happened today...

1. _____

2. _____

3. _____

How did I make these things happen?

_____

_____

_____

DATE: ____/____/____

I am grateful for...

1. _____
2. _____
3. _____

My goals for today are...

1. _____
2. _____
3. _____

My motivation for today is...

_____

_____

These wonderful things happened today...

1. _____
2. _____
3. _____

How did I make these things happen?

_____

_____

_____

DATE: _____/_____/_____

I am grateful for...

1._____

2._____

3._____

My goals for today are...

1._____

2._____

3._____

My motivation for today is...

_____

_____

These wonderful things happened today...

1._____

2._____

3._____

How did I make these things happen?

_____

_____

_____

DATE: _____/_____/_____

I am grateful for...

1. _____

2. _____

3. _____

My goals for today are...

1. _____

2. _____

3. _____

My motivation for today is...

_____

_____

These wonderful things happened today...

1. _____

2. _____

3. _____

How did I make these things happen?

_____

_____

_____

DATE: ____/____/____

I am grateful for...

1. _____
2. _____
3. _____

My goals for today are...

1. _____
2. _____
3. _____

My motivation for today is...

_____

_____

These wonderful things happened today...

1. _____
2. _____
3. _____

How did I make these things happen?

_____

_____

_____

DATE: _____/_____/_____

I am grateful for...

1. _____

2. _____

3. _____

My goals for today are...

1. _____

2. _____

3. _____

My motivation for today is...

_____

_____

These wonderful things happened today...

1. _____

2. _____

3. _____

How did I make these things happen?

_____

_____

_____

DATE: _____/_____/_____

I am grateful for...

1. _____
2. _____
3. _____

My goals for today are...

1. _____
2. _____
3. _____

My motivation for today is...

_____

_____

These wonderful things happened today...

1. _____
2. _____
3. _____

How did I make these things happen?

_____

_____

_____

DATE: _____ / _____ / _____

I am grateful for...

1. _____

2. _____

3. _____

My goals for today are...

1. _____

2. _____

3. _____

My motivation for today is...

_____

_____

These wonderful things happened today...

1. _____

2. _____

3. _____

How did I make these things happen?

_____

_____

_____

DATE: _____/_____/_____

I am grateful for...

1. _____
2. _____
3. _____

My goals for today are...

1. _____
2. _____
3. _____

My motivation for today is...

_____

_____

These wonderful things happened today...

1. _____
2. _____
3. _____

How did I make these things happen?

_____

_____

_____

DATE: ____/____/____

I am grateful for...

1. _____
2. _____
3. _____

My goals for today are...

1. _____
2. _____
3. _____

My motivation for today is...

_____

_____

These wonderful things happened today...

1. _____
2. _____
3. _____

How did I make these things happen?

_____

_____

_____

DATE: _____/_____/_____

I am grateful for...

1._____
2._____
3._____

My goals for today are...

1._____
2._____
3._____

My motivation for today is...

_____

_____

These wonderful things happened today...

1._____
2._____
3._____

How did I make these things happen?

_____

_____

_____

DATE: _____/_____/_____

I am grateful for...

1. _____
2. _____
3. _____

My goals for today are...

1. _____
2. _____
3. _____

My motivation for today is...

_____

_____

These wonderful things happened today...

1. _____
2. _____
3. _____

How did I make these things happen?

_____

_____

_____

DATE: ____/____/____

I am grateful for...

1._____
2._____
3._____

My goals for today are...

1._____
2._____
3._____

My motivation for today is...

_____

_____

These wonderful things happened today...

1._____
2._____
3._____

How did I make these things happen?

_____

_____

_____

DATE: _____/_____/_____

I am grateful for...

1. _____
2. _____
3. _____

My goals for today are...

1. _____
2. _____
3. _____

My motivation for today is...

_____

_____

These wonderful things happened today...

1. _____
2. _____
3. _____

How did I make these things happen?

_____

_____

_____

DATE: _____ / _____ / _____

I am grateful for...

1. _____
2. _____
3. _____

My goals for today are...

1. _____
2. _____
3. _____

My motivation for today is...

_____

_____

These wonderful things happened today...

1. _____
2. _____
3. _____

How did I make these things happen?

_____

_____

_____

DATE: _____/_____/_____

I am grateful for...

1. _____

2. _____

3. _____

My goals for today are...

1. _____

2. _____

3. _____

My motivation for today is...

_____

_____

These wonderful things happened today...

1. _____

2. _____

3. _____

How did I make these things happen?

_____

_____

_____

DATE: ____/____/____

I am grateful for...

1. _____

2. _____

3. _____

My goals for today are...

1. _____

2. _____

3. _____

My motivation for today is...

_____

_____

These wonderful things happened today...

1. _____

2. _____

3. _____

How did I make these things happen?

_____

_____

_____

DATE: ____ / ____ / ____

I am grateful for...

1. _____
2. _____
3. _____

My goals for today are...

1. _____
2. _____
3. _____

My motivation for today is...

_____

_____

These wonderful things happened today...

1. _____
2. _____
3. _____

How did I make these things happen?

_____

_____

_____

DATE: ____/____/____

I am grateful for...

1. _____

2. _____

3. _____

My goals for today are...

1. _____

2. _____

3. _____

My motivation for today is...

_____

_____

These wonderful things happened today...

1. _____

2. _____

3. _____

How did I make these things happen?

_____

_____

_____

DATE: _____/_____/_____

I am grateful for...

1. _____
2. _____
3. _____

My goals for today are...

1. _____
2. _____
3. _____

My motivation for today is...

_____

_____

These wonderful things happened today...

1. _____
2. _____
3. _____

How did I make these things happen?

_____

_____

_____

DATE: ____/____/____

I am grateful for...

1. _____
2. _____
3. _____

My goals for today are...

1. _____
2. _____
3. _____

My motivation for today is...

_____

_____

These wonderful things happened today...

1. _____
2. _____
3. _____

How did I make these things happen?

_____

_____

_____

DATE: _____ / _____ / _____

I am grateful for...

1. _____
2. _____
3. _____

My goals for today are...

1. _____
2. _____
3. _____

My motivation for today is...

_____

_____

These wonderful things happened today...

1. _____
2. _____
3. _____

How did I make these things happen?

_____

_____

_____

DATE: _____/_____/_____

I am grateful for...

1. _____

2. _____

3. _____

My goals for today are...

1. _____

2. _____

3. _____

My motivation for today is...

_____

_____

These wonderful things happened today...

1. _____

2. _____

3. _____

How did I make these things happen?

_____

_____

_____

DATE: ____/____/____

I am grateful for...

1. _____
2. _____
3. _____

My goals for today are...

1. _____
2. _____
3. _____

My motivation for today is...

_____

_____

These wonderful things happened today...

1. _____
2. _____
3. _____

How did I make these things happen?

_____

_____

_____

DATE: _____/_____/_____

I am grateful for...

1._____

2._____

3._____

My goals for today are...

1._____

2._____

3._____

My motivation for today is...

_____

_____

These wonderful things happened today...

1._____

2._____

3._____

How did I make these things happen?

_____

_____

_____

DATE: _____ / _____ / _____

I am grateful for...

1. _____

2. _____

3. _____

My goals for today are...

1. _____

2. _____

3. _____

My motivation for today is...

_____

_____

These wonderful things happened today...

1. _____

2. _____

3. _____

How did I make these things happen?

_____

_____

_____

DATE: _____/_____/_____

I am grateful for...

1._____
2._____
3._____

My goals for today are...

1._____
2._____
3._____

My motivation for today is...

_____

_____

These wonderful things happened today...

1._____
2._____
3._____

How did I make these things happen?

_____

_____

_____

DATE: _____/_____/_____

I am grateful for...

1. _____
2. _____
3. _____

My goals for today are...

1. _____
2. _____
3. _____

My motivation for today is...

_____

_____

These wonderful things happened today...

1. _____
2. _____
3. _____

How did I make these things happen?

_____

_____

_____

DATE: ____/____/____

I am grateful for...

1. _____
2. _____
3. _____

My goals for today are...

1. _____
2. _____
3. _____

My motivation for today is...

_____

_____

These wonderful things happened today...

1. _____
2. _____
3. _____

How did I make these things happen?

_____

_____

_____

DATE: _____/_____/_____

I am grateful for...

1. _____
2. _____
3. _____

My goals for today are...

1. _____
2. _____
3. _____

My motivation for today is...

_____

_____

These wonderful things happened today...

1. _____
2. _____
3. _____

How did I make these things happen?

_____

_____

_____

DATE: _____/_____/_____

I am grateful for...

1. _____
2. _____
3. _____

My goals for today are...

1. _____
2. _____
3. _____

My motivation for today is...

_____

_____

These wonderful things happened today...

1. _____
2. _____
3. _____

How did I make these things happen?

_____

_____

_____

DATE: _____/_____/_____

I am grateful for...

1. _____
2. _____
3. _____

My goals for today are...

1. _____
2. _____
3. _____

My motivation for today is...

_____

_____

These wonderful things happened today...

1. _____
2. _____
3. _____

How did I make these things happen?

_____

_____

_____

DATE: ____/____/____

I am grateful for...

1._____
2._____
3._____

My goals for today are...

1._____
2._____
3._____

My motivation for today is...

_____

_____

These wonderful things happened today...

1._____
2._____
3._____

How did I make these things happen?

_____

_____

_____

DATE: ____/____/____

I am grateful for...

1. _____
2. _____
3. _____

My goals for today are...

1. _____
2. _____
3. _____

My motivation for today is...

_____

_____

These wonderful things happened today...

1. _____
2. _____
3. _____

How did I make these things happen?

_____

_____

_____

DATE: ____/____/____

I am grateful for...

1._____

2._____

3._____

My goals for today are...

1._____

2._____

3._____

My motivation for today is...

_____

_____

These wonderful things happened today...

1._____

2._____

3._____

How did I make these things happen?

_____

_____

_____

DATE: ____/____/____

I am grateful for...

1. _____

2. _____

3. _____

My goals for today are...

1. _____

2. _____

3. _____

My motivation for today is...

_____

_____

These wonderful things happened today...

1. _____

2. _____

3. _____

How did I make these things happen?

_____

_____

_____

DATE: _____/_____/_____

I am grateful for...

1. _____
2. _____
3. _____

My goals for today are...

1. _____
2. _____
3. _____

My motivation for today is...

_____

_____

These wonderful things happened today...

1. _____
2. _____
3. _____

How did I make these things happen?

_____

_____

_____

DATE: _____/_____/_____

I am grateful for...

1. _____
2. _____
3. _____

My goals for today are...

1. _____
2. _____
3. _____

My motivation for today is...

_____

_____

These wonderful things happened today...

1. _____
2. _____
3. _____

How did I make these things happen?

_____

_____

_____

DATE: _____/_____/_____

I am grateful for...

1._____

2._____

3._____

My goals for today are...

1._____

2._____

3._____

My motivation for today is...

_____

_____

These wonderful things happened today...

1._____

2._____

3._____

How did I make these things happen?

_____

_____

_____

DATE: _____/_____/_____

I am grateful for...

1. _____
2. _____
3. _____

My goals for today are...

1. _____
2. _____
3. _____

My motivation for today is...

_____

_____

These wonderful things happened today...

1. _____
2. _____
3. _____

How did I make these things happen?

_____

_____

_____

DATE: _____/_____/_____

I am grateful for...

1. _____
2. _____
3. _____

My goals for today are...

1. _____
2. _____
3. _____

My motivation for today is...

_____

_____

These wonderful things happened today...

1. _____
2. _____
3. _____

How did I make these things happen?

_____

_____

_____

DATE: _____ / _____ / _____

I am grateful for...

1. _____

2. _____

3. _____

My goals for today are...

1. _____

2. _____

3. _____

My motivation for today is...

_____

_____

These wonderful things happened today...

1. _____

2. _____

3. _____

How did I make these things happen?

_____

_____

_____

DATE: _____/_____/_____

I am grateful for...

1. _____
2. _____
3. _____

My goals for today are...

1. _____
2. _____
3. _____

My motivation for today is...

_____

_____

These wonderful things happened today...

1. _____
2. _____
3. _____

How did I make these things happen?

_____

_____

_____

DATE: ____ / ____ / ____

I am grateful for...

1. _____
2. _____
3. _____

My goals for today are...

1. _____
2. _____
3. _____

My motivation for today is...

_____

_____

These wonderful things happened today...

1. _____
2. _____
3. _____

How did I make these things happen?

_____

_____

_____

DATE: _____/_____/_____

I am grateful for...

1._____

2._____

3._____

My goals for today are...

1._____

2._____

3._____

My motivation for today is...

_____

_____

These wonderful things happened today...

1._____

2._____

3._____

How did I make these things happen?

_____

_____

_____

DATE: _____/_____/_____

I am grateful for...

1. _____
2. _____
3. _____

My goals for today are...

1. _____
2. _____
3. _____

My motivation for today is...

_____

_____

These wonderful things happened today...

1. _____
2. _____
3. _____

How did I make these things happen?

_____

_____

_____

DATE: ____/____/____

I am grateful for...

1._____
2._____
3._____

My goals for today are...

1._____
2._____
3._____

My motivation for today is...

_____

_____

These wonderful things happened today...

1._____
2._____
3._____

How did I make these things happen?

_____

_____

_____

DATE: ____/____/____

I am grateful for...

1. _____
2. _____
3. _____

My goals for today are...

1. _____
2. _____
3. _____

My motivation for today is...

_____

_____

These wonderful things happened today...

1. _____
2. _____
3. _____

How did I make these things happen?

_____

_____

_____

DATE: ____/____/____

I am grateful for...

1. _____
2. _____
3. _____

My goals for today are...

1. _____
2. _____
3. _____

My motivation for today is...

_____

_____

These wonderful things happened today...

1. _____
2. _____
3. _____

How did I make these things happen?

_____

_____

_____

DATE: _____/_____/_____

I am grateful for...

1._____
2._____
3._____

My goals for today are...

1._____
2._____
3._____

My motivation for today is...

_____

_____

These wonderful things happened today...

1._____
2._____
3._____

How did I make these things happen?

_____

_____

_____

DATE: ____/____/____

I am grateful for...

1. _____
2. _____
3. _____

My goals for today are...

1. _____
2. _____
3. _____

My motivation for today is...

_____

_____

These wonderful things happened today...

1. _____
2. _____
3. _____

How did I make these things happen?

_____

_____

_____

DATE: _____/_____/_____

I am grateful for...

1. _____
2. _____
3. _____

My goals for today are...

1. _____
2. _____
3. _____

My motivation for today is...

_____

_____

These wonderful things happened today...

1. _____
2. _____
3. _____

How did I make these things happen?

_____

_____

_____

DATE: ____/____/____

I am grateful for...

1._____

2._____

3._____

My goals for today are...

1._____

2._____

3._____

My motivation for today is...

_____

_____

These wonderful things happened today...

1._____

2._____

3._____

How did I make these things happen?

_____

_____

_____

DATE: _____/_____/_____

I am grateful for...

1. _____
2. _____
3. _____

My goals for today are...

1. _____
2. _____
3. _____

My motivation for today is...

_____

_____

These wonderful things happened today...

1. _____
2. _____
3. _____

How did I make these things happen?

_____

_____

_____

DATE: _____/_____/_____

I am grateful for...

1. _____

2. _____

3. _____

My goals for today are...

1. _____

2. _____

3. _____

My motivation for today is...

_____

_____

These wonderful things happened today...

1. _____

2. _____

3. _____

How did I make these things happen?

_____

_____

_____

DATE: ____/____/____

I am grateful for...

1. _____
2. _____
3. _____

My goals for today are...

1. _____
2. _____
3. _____

My motivation for today is...

_____

_____

These wonderful things happened today...

1. _____
2. _____
3. _____

How did I make these things happen?

_____

_____

_____

DATE: _____/_____/_____

I am grateful for...

1. _____
2. _____
3. _____

My goals for today are...

1. _____
2. _____
3. _____

My motivation for today is...

_____

_____

These wonderful things happened today...

1. _____
2. _____
3. _____

How did I make these things happen?

_____

_____

_____

DATE: ____/____/____

I am grateful for...

1. _____
2. _____
3. _____

My goals for today are...

1. _____
2. _____
3. _____

My motivation for today is...

_____

_____

These wonderful things happened today...

1. _____
2. _____
3. _____

How did I make these things happen?

_____

_____

_____

DATE: _____/_____/_____

I am grateful for...

1. _____
2. _____
3. _____

My goals for today are...

1. _____
2. _____
3. _____

My motivation for today is...

_____

_____

These wonderful things happened today...

1. _____
2. _____
3. _____

How did I make these things happen?

_____

_____

_____

DATE: _____/_____/_____

I am grateful for...

1. _____

2. _____

3. _____

My goals for today are...

1. _____

2. _____

3. _____

My motivation for today is...

_____

_____

These wonderful things happened today...

1. _____

2. _____

3. _____

How did I make these things happen?

_____

_____

_____

DATE: ____/____/____

I am grateful for...

1._____

2._____

3._____

My goals for today are...

1._____

2._____

3._____

My motivation for today is...

_____

_____

These wonderful things happened today...

1._____

2._____

3._____

How did I make these things happen?

_____

_____

_____

DATE: ____/____/____

I am grateful for...

1. _____
2. _____
3. _____

My goals for today are...

1. _____
2. _____
3. _____

My motivation for today is...

_____

_____

These wonderful things happened today...

1. _____
2. _____
3. _____

How did I make these things happen?

_____

_____

_____

DATE: ____ / ____ / ____

I am grateful for...

1. _____
2. _____
3. _____

My goals for today are...

1. _____
2. _____
3. _____

My motivation for today is...

_____

_____

These wonderful things happened today...

1. _____
2. _____
3. _____

How did I make these things happen?

_____

_____

_____

DATE: ____/____/____

I am grateful for...

1. _____
2. _____
3. _____

My goals for today are...

1. _____
2. _____
3. _____

My motivation for today is...

_____

_____

These wonderful things happened today...

1. _____
2. _____
3. _____

How did I make these things happen?

_____

_____

_____

DATE: _____/_____/_____

I am grateful for...

1._____

2._____

3._____

My goals for today are...

1._____

2._____

3._____

My motivation for today is...

_____

_____

These wonderful things happened today...

1._____

2._____

3._____

How did I make these things happen?

_____

_____

_____

DATE: ____/____/____

I am grateful for...

1. _____
2. _____
3. _____

My goals for today are...

1. _____
2. _____
3. _____

My motivation for today is...

_____

_____

These wonderful things happened today...

1. _____
2. _____
3. _____

How did I make these things happen?

_____

_____

_____

DATE: ____/____/____

I am grateful for...

1. _____
2. _____
3. _____

My goals for today are...

1. _____
2. _____
3. _____

My motivation for today is...

_____

_____

These wonderful things happened today...

1. _____
2. _____
3. _____

How did I make these things happen?

_____

_____

_____

DATE: _____/_____/_____

I am grateful for...

1. _____
2. _____
3. _____

My goals for today are...

1. _____
2. _____
3. _____

My motivation for today is...

_____

_____

These wonderful things happened today...

1. _____
2. _____
3. _____

How did I make these things happen?

_____

_____

_____

DATE: _____/_____/_____

I am grateful for...

1._____

2._____

3._____

My goals for today are...

1._____

2._____

3._____

My motivation for today is...

_____

_____

These wonderful things happened today...

1._____

2._____

3._____

How did I make these things happen?

_____

_____

_____

DATE: _____/_____/_____

I am grateful for...

1._____
2._____
3._____

My goals for today are...

1._____
2._____
3._____

My motivation for today is...

_____

_____

These wonderful things happened today...

1._____
2._____
3._____

How did I make these things happen?

_____

_____

_____

DATE: _____/_____/_____

I am grateful for...

1._____
2._____
3._____

My goals for today are...

1._____
2._____
3._____

My motivation for today is...

_____

_____

These wonderful things happened today...

1._____
2._____
3._____

How did I make these things happen?

_____

_____

_____

DATE: ____/____/____

I am grateful for...

1. _____

2. _____

3. _____

My goals for today are...

1. _____

2. _____

3. _____

My motivation for today is...

_____

_____

These wonderful things happened today...

1. _____

2. _____

3. _____

How did I make these things happen?

_____

_____

_____

DATE: ____/____/____

I am grateful for...

1. _____
2. _____
3. _____

My goals for today are...

1. _____
2. _____
3. _____

My motivation for today is...

_____

_____

These wonderful things happened today...

1. _____
2. _____
3. _____

How did I make these things happen?

_____

_____

_____

DATE: ____/____/____

I am grateful for...

1. _____
2. _____
3. _____

My goals for today are...

1. _____
2. _____
3. _____

My motivation for today is...

_____

_____

These wonderful things happened today...

1. _____
2. _____
3. _____

How did I make these things happen?

_____

_____

_____

DATE: _____/_____/_____

I am grateful for...

1._____

2._____

3._____

My goals for today are...

1._____

2._____

3._____

My motivation for today is...

_____

_____

These wonderful things happened today...

1._____

2._____

3._____

How did I make these things happen?

_____

_____

_____

DATE: _____ / _____ / _____

I am grateful for...

1. _____
2. _____
3. _____

My goals for today are...

1. _____
2. _____
3. _____

My motivation for today is...

_____

_____

These wonderful things happened today...

1. _____
2. _____
3. _____

How did I make these things happen?

_____

_____

_____

DATE: _____/_____/_____

I am grateful for...

1._____

2._____

3._____

My goals for today are...

1._____

2._____

3._____

My motivation for today is...

_____

_____

These wonderful things happened today...

1._____

2._____

3._____

How did I make these things happen?

_____

_____

_____

Made in the USA
San Bernardino, CA
13 June 2017